Tinkle, Tinkle, Little Tot

Songs & Rhymes for Toilet Training

Bruce Lansky,
Robert Pottle, and Friends
Illustrated by Anne Catharine Blake

Meadowbrook Press

Distributed by Simon & Schuster
New York

Poem	Author	Page

Foreword

Toilet training should not be a daunting or dreaded task.
This enjoyable book of songs and rhymes helps parents and
children discuss common toilet training issues in an entertaining
and motivational way. *Tinkle, Tinkle, Little Tot* provides a practical
and novel way to help children master good bathroom habits.
This book makes toilet training fun!

D. Preston Smith, MD, FAAP, FACS, FSPU
Pediatric Urologist; Author, *The Potty Trainer*; Founder, PottyMD.com

Author's Note

This book contains fifteen songs and three rhymes.
Most parents enjoy singing the songs and reciting the rhymes.
However, if you'd like to sing all three rhymes, too, try singing
"Star Light, Star Bright" to the tune "Twinkle, Twinkle, Little Star."
"Piddle Diddle" can be sung to the tune of "Diddle, Diddle Dumpling"
if you know it or "Twinkle, Twinkle, Little Star." And "Toilet Paper Squares"
can be sung to the tune of "Hush, Little Baby" or "Twinkle, Twinkle, Little Star."

Happy toilet training!

Bruce Lansky

My New Potty

(to the tune of "My Bonnie")

I can't wait to use my new potty
When we get it home from the store.
I'll pee and I'll poop in the potty.
No diapers for me anymore.

I can't wait to use my new potty
When I have to poo-poo or pee.
I'll hop, skip, and jump to the bathroom.
The potty is where I will be.

The Pee-Pee Dance [*]

(to the tune of "The Hokey Pokey")

You cross your right foot left.
You cross your left foot right.
You squeeze your knees together,
And you hold them really tight.
You tiptoe to the potty
So you will not wet your pants.
You're doing the Pee-Pee Dance.

You make a little jump.
You make a little hop.
You squeeze your knees together,
And you know you shouldn't stop.
Keep hopping to the potty
'Cause you cannot take a chance.
You're doing the Pee-Pee Dance.

[*]To do the Pee-Pee Dance, have your toddler act out the movements in each line. For the lines "You squeeze

your knees together" and "You're doing the Pee-Pee Dance," have your toddler wiggle from side to side.

Piddle Diddle

Diddle diddle dumpling, my son John
Went to the potty with his blue jeans on.
The zipper got stuck, gave John a scare—
He piddled in a puddle in his underwear.

Hush, Little Darling
(to the tune of "Hush, Little Baby")

Hush, little darling,
Don't you fret.
Let's clean up–
Your pants are wet.

Hush, little darling,
Don't you cry.
Someday soon
You will stay dry.

Tinkle, Tinkle, Little Tot

(to the tune of "Twinkle, Twinkle, Little Star")

Tinkle, tinkle, little tot, sitting there upon the pot.
Any second now, you'll see...sprinkle, splash, you'll go pee-pee!
Tinkle, tinkle, little tot, sitting there upon the pot.

Tinkle, Tinkle, Little Star

(to the tune of "Twinkle, Twinkle, Little Star")

Tinkle, tinkle, little star, what a potty pro you are!
Perched upon your potty chair, you know how to pee-pee there.
Tinkle, tinkle, little star, what a potty pro you are!

The Tushy Pushy

(to the tune of "The Hokey Pokey")

You pull your undies down.
You take the potty out.
You sit your bottom down,
And you push the poopy out.
You do the Tushy Pushy
Till the poop is in the pot.
That's what it's all about!

Itsy-Bitsy Poo-Poo

(to the tune of "Itsy-Bitsy Spider")

An itsy-bitsy poo-poo
Was floating in the bowl.
I wiped my bum with paper
And flushed it down the hole.

I washed my hands with soap,
Then I walked right out the door.
And I'll return again
When I have to poop some more.

If You Pee-Peed in the Potty

(to the tune of "If You're Happy and You Know It")

If you pee-peed in the potty, shout "Hooray."
Hooray!
If you pee-peed in the potty, shout "Hooray."
Hooray!
If you gave it your best shot
And your pee is in the pot,
If you pee-peed in the potty, shout "Hooray."
Hooray!

If You Poo-Pooed in the Potty

(to the tune of "If You're Happy and You Know It")

If you poo-pooed in the potty, shout "Hooray."
Hooray!
If you poo-pooed in the potty, shout "Hooray."
Hooray!
If you pushed a poo-poo out,
Then you really ought to shout.
If you poo-pooed in the potty, shout "Hooray."
Hooray!

Toilet Paper Squares

One square, two square, three square, four—
Do not sprinkle on the floor.
Five square, six square, seven square, eight—
Flush the toilet, you did great!

If You Sprinkle

(to the tune of "Alouette")

If you sprinkle when you go to tinkle,
please be neat and wipe the toilet seat.

In the bathroom please be neat.
If you sprinkle, wipe the seat.
Please be neat. (Please be neat.)
Wipe the seat. (Wipe the seat.)
Ohhhhhh!

If you sprinkle when you go to tinkle,
please be neat and wipe the toilet seat.

17

Wipe with Paper
(to the tune of "Frère Jacques")

Wipe with paper.
Wipe with paper.
Flush it down.
Flush it down.

Wash with soap and water.
Wash with soap and water.
Dry your hands.
Dry your hands.

19

This Is the Way
(to the tune of "The Mulberry Bush")

This is the way we wash our hands,
Wash our hands, wash our hands.
This is the way we wash our hands
After using the potty.

20

Wet our hands and soap them up.
Rub, rub, rub, and clean them up.
Rinse our hands and dry them up
After using the potty.

I Can
(to the tune of "This Old Man")

I can poop,
I can pee,
In the toilet.
Yes, sirree!
I can flush the potty and
Wash up when I'm done.
Going potty sure is fun!

Humpty Dumpty Sat on the Pot

(to the tune of "Humpty Dumpty")

Humpty Dumpty sat on the pot.
Humpty Dumpty tinkled a lot.
Now all the king's horses
And all the king's men
Will never dress Humpty in diapers again.

Time to Pee

(to the tune of "Frère Jacques")

It's your bedtime.
It's your bedtime.
Time to pee.
Time to pee.

Peeing in the potty,
Peeing in the potty,
Helps you stay
Dry all night.

Star Light, Star Bright

Star light, star bright,
First star I see tonight,
I'm going to try with all my might
To keep my jammies dry all night.

Library of Congress Cataloging-in-Publication Data

Lansky, Bruce.

  Tinkle, tinkle, little tot : songs and rhymes for toilet training / by Bruce Lansky, Robert Pottle, and Friends ; illustrated by Anne Catharine Blake.
      p. cm.

  Summary: "Songs and rhymes to encourage and motivate your toddler during the toilet-training process"--Provided by publisher.

  ISBN 0-88166-492-8 (Meadowbrook) ISBN 0-689-04646-4 (Simon & Schuster)

  1. Toilet training--Juvenile literature. 2. Children's songs--Juvenile literature. 3. Singing games--Juvenile literature. I. Pottle, Robert.

II. Blake, Anne Catharine. III. Title.

  HQ770.5.L34 2005

  649'.62--dc22

                              2005005480

Coordinating Editor and Copyeditor: Angela Wiechmann

Production Manager: Paul Woods

Graphic Design Manager: Tamara Peterson

Illustrations and Cover Art: Anne Catharine Blake

Published by Meadowbrook Press, 5451 Smetana Drive, Minnetonka, Minnesota 55343

www.meadowbrookpress.com

BOOK TRADE DISTRIBUTION by Simon and Schuster, a division of Simon and Schuster, Inc., 1230 Avenue of the Americas, New York, New York 10020

10 09 08 07 06 05   10 9 8 7 6 5 4 3 2 1

Printed in Hong Kong